John Locke

Philosopher of the Enlightenment

Patrice Sherman

Publishing Credits

Dona Herweck Rice, *Editor-in-Chief*
Lee Aucoin, *Creative Director*
Torrey Maloof, *Editor*
Neri Garcia, *Senior Designer*
Stephanie Reid, *Photo Researcher*
Rachelle Cracchiolo, M.S.Ed., *Publisher*

Image Credits

Teacher Created Materials

5301 Oceanus Drive
Huntington Beach, CA 92649-1030
http://www.tcmpub.com
ISBN 978-1-4333-5014-6

Table of Contents

John Locke: The Quiet Revolutionary

In 1689, John Locke (lok) returned to London, England. He was 57 years old. He had spent the past few years living in the Netherlands. Locke was glad to be home. London was one of the most powerful and exciting cities in Europe.

Two years earlier, in 1687, Isaac (AHY-zuhk) Newton had published his three laws of motion. These laws changed the study of physics. Architect Christopher Wren (ren) was in the process of changing the city. He was building Saint Paul's Cathedral. In 1688, the Glorious **Revolution** changed England's government. The revolution drove King James II from the throne and introduced the country's first Bill of Rights.

John Locke

Saint Paul's Cathedral

Christopher Wren

Christopher Wren's skill with measurement inspired him to take up architecture. In 1666, the Great Fire destroyed 80 percent of London. The king asked Wren to assist with rebuilding 51 of the city's churches. Saint Paul's Cathedral is considered Wren's masterpiece.

Sir Isaac Newton

Isaac Newton excelled in almost every subject he studied. He was a mathematician, an astronomer, a physicist, a chemist, and a geologist. In his spare time, he studied religion. He built telescopes and performed experiments to show the effects of gravity. In 1687, he established his *Three Universal Laws of Motion*. These laws became the basis for modern physics.

Locke lived in an age of great change called the **Enlightenment** (en-LAHYT-n-muhnt). But he was not a scientist or an architect. Locke was a **philosopher**. He spent most of his time thinking and writing. His favorite subject was the human mind. How did people learn? How did they know what was true? More importantly, how could they live together? Locke was a thinker and a quiet man, and his thoughts were about to change the world.

This is the cottage in Somerset, England, where Locke was born.

Locke the Young Scholar

The Two Lockes

Locke was born in a peaceful corner of England in 1632. His hometown of Pensford, in North Somerset, England, was a **rural** area. It was known for sheep farming.

Locke was named after his father, John Locke, Senior. The older Locke worked as a lawyer and **clerk** to the local justices. He enjoyed reading in his spare time. He also kept a journal. In it he recorded the names of some of his favorite books. These included histories and **sermons**. Locke's father also made notes on plants that could be used for medicine.

After he grew up, John Locke remembered his father as a stern but kind man. The two shared many traits. Like his father, Locke kept journals throughout his life. In school, he studied medicine. Outside school, Locke read widely. He enjoyed poetry, **philosophy**, and natural history.

Above all, his father taught Locke to value education. The older Locke hoped that his son would become a scholar. Locke would fulfill his father's dreams. First, however, he had to face a war that would change everything in England.

Cromwell leads British troops in the English Civil War.

The English Civil War

In 1642, war broke out in England between the Roundheads, or Parliamentarians (pahr-luh-men-TAIR-ee-uhnz), and the Cavaliers (kav-uh-LEERS). The Cavaliers believed in the absolute power of the king. The Roundheads believed that the highest power in the land should belong to Parliament. The Parliamentarians won. In 1649, they beheaded King Charles I and declared England a commonwealth under the leadership of Oliver Cromwell.

Roundheads and Cavaliers

The Roundheads got their name because they wore simple round-brimmed hats instead of the fancy hats worn by the rich. The word *Cavalier* comes from the French word for horseman. Cavaliers rode horses and wore fancy attire to display their wealth.

The Storm of War

The English Civil War broke out in 1642. Locke was only 10 years old. The war would last until he was 19. His father sided with the Parliamentarians, who were against the king. The senior Locke left his law practice and joined the Parliamentarian army as a captain.

Fighting grew fierce in Somerset. Many rebels had their homes burned to the ground by the king's forces. The Locke family did not lose their house, but they did suffer financial losses. Young John Locke saw that his father was willing to make sacrifices for a cause in which he believed.

(201)   Numb. 26

A Perfect Diuinall

OF SOME

PASSAGES
IN
PARLIAMENT:

And from other parts of this Kingdom, from Munday the
15. of *Iannary*, till Munday the 22. of *Iannary*, *Anno* 1643.

Collected for the satisfaction of such as desire to be truly informed.

Printed for *Francis Coles* and *Laurence Blaikelock* : And are to be sold
at their Shops in the *Old-Baily*, and at *Temple-Bar*.

Munday the 15. of January.

Here was a Conference of both Houses this morning, upon occasion of a Letter from the Lord *Roberts* to his Excellency the Earle of *Essex*, for some supplies of money for the Army, which was left to the consideration of the Commons. And they accordingly taking the same into consideration, agreed in an order for the speedy raising of 10000 pound, out of the profits of the Excise Office, or to be procured upon loane for the present supply of the Army, untill such time as the said summe can be raised out of the Excise Office. And they appointed a Committee to treat with the Commissioners for Excise this afternoone about the same.

There was also another Conference of the Houses about the Earle of *Holland*, touching which the Lords gave the Commons to understand, that they have been often sollicited by petition and otherwaies, for the restoration of the said Earle of *Holland* to his place in their House againe ; and more particularly, received a petition on the Saturday before by the Noble Admirall the Earle of *Warwicke* in his behalfe; with much submission acknowledging his errour for his former deserting the Parliament , upon the grounds and reasons faithfully related , in his

With a true relation of a great victory lately obtained by Sir *Wil, Brereton* and Sir *Tho. Fair*, six against the enemy neere *Nampwich*, in which fight there were 1600 of the enemies killed and taken prisoners, great store of Armes 14 Colours, 7 carriages, and other rich prize.

Cc   exa-

A printed newspaper reporting the proceedings of Parliament during the English Civil War.

Cromwell refuses the crown.

As an adult, Locke wrote that he had scarcely begun to grow up when he found himself in the middle of a storm. This storm would go on for nearly 40 years. The end of the English Civil War in 1651 did not bring an end to conflict. The issues still sparked debate. People wondered which kind of government was best. How much power should a single ruler have? What was the role of Parliament? Still in his teens, Locke thought about these questions, too. He did not yet realize that answering them would be his life's work.

A Peregrine Takes Flight

Locke was able to spend most of the Civil War away from the violence. At the age of 14, he entered Westminster School. This was a **prestigious** boarding school in England. At school, he was called a peregrine (PER-i-grin). A peregrine is a migrating bird. It was the name given to country boys who had traveled a great distance to attend school.

Life at school was hard. Students rose at five in the morning. The daily schedule consisted of prayers, classes, and brief meals, followed by more prayers and classes. All classes in history and literature were taught in **Latin**. Other subjects included Greek, Hebrew, and Arabic. Locke also studied geography and geometry. Students were expected to memorize long texts. They could be whipped for breaking any of the rules. Locke hated this use of physical discipline.

Locke's own ideas of education would become quite different. He did not like Westminster. He did well though. He even won a King's **Scholarship** in 1650. This was a very high honor. It gave Locke money to buy more books for school. When Locke finished his studies at Westminster, he entered Oxford (OKS-ferd) University. The peregrine was taking flight.

Rhetoric

In Locke's day, all students were expected to learn rhetoric. *Rhetoric* is the art of speaking and writing effectively. Locke did not object to rhetoric. However, he did think that students were often asked to speak on subjects they knew very little about. He compared this to being asked to make bricks without any materials to do so.

John Dryden

One of Locke's fellow students at Westminster was the poet and playwright John Dryden. In 1667, King Charles II named Dryden poet laureate (LAWR-ee-it), the official poet of the nation.

John Dryden

peregrine falcon

school room of Westminster

Latin and Law

As with Westminster, almost all the classes at Oxford University were taught in Latin. Students were also expected to speak Latin at dinner. If they spoke to one another outside of class, they had to speak in Latin as well. Locke felt bored and did not do well in his classes.

Locke lacked interest in his studies, but he was eager to make friends. He found several young men who liked discussing politics, science, and philosophy. During breaks, they exchanged letters with one another. Writing letters gave Locke a chance to develop some of his own ideas.

Oxford University

Locke graduated in 1658. He then went to London to study law. After a year, however, he returned to Oxford to study medicine. From 1659 to 1667, he pursued a medical degree. He also worked as a tutor helping other students. He had now found an academic life that suited him. His new friend, the chemist Robert Boyle, introduced Locke to the scientific revolution. Locke quickly turned his attention from the laws of man to those of nature.

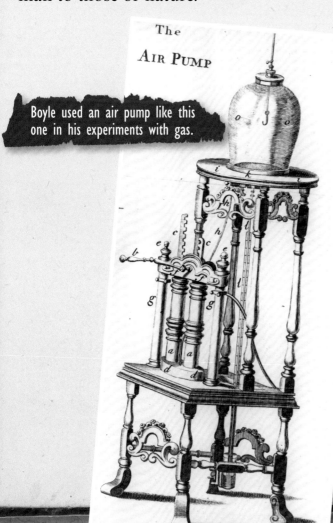

The AIR PUMP

Boyle used an air pump like this one in his experiments with gas.

Robert Boyle

A Turning Point

A Natural Philosopher

Since his childhood, Locke had kept journals. They were filled with ideas and quotes from the books he read. In the 1660s, he started adding notes on the weather. He thought the weather might cause certain diseases. Locke hoped his notes would be useful to other doctors.

Locke's friend Robert Boyle taught him how to use a **barometer** (buh-ROM-i-ter). Locke wanted to measure the air pressure in lead mines. He wondered if the miners suffered from a lack of fresh air. But the miners were suspicious of the device and would not let Locke into the mine.

Locke was very interested in human **respiration**. He became convinced that breathing brought a life-giving substance to the blood. Later researchers identified that substance as oxygen.

seventeenth-century barometers

In 1667, Locke moved into the London home of Lord Anthony Ashley-Cooper, the Earl of Shaftesbury. Locke served as the earl's personal doctor. There, he met Thomas Sydenham (SAI-den-hahm). Sydenham was one of England's leading doctors. Together they performed a life-saving operation on the earl. The two removed a growth from his liver. The earl was so grateful that he became Locke's **patron**. He gave Locke money so that he could devote more time to his studies.

The Scientific Revolution

Most historians agree that the scientific revolution started in 1543, when Copernicus (koh-PUR-ni-kuhs) declared that Earth revolved around the sun. In the 1600s, scientists began to use observations, measurements, and experiments to investigate nature. Major figures included astronomer Galileo (gal-uh-LEY-oh) and physicist Isaac Newton.

Thomas Sydenham

Sydenham is one of the founders of modern medicine. He studied the symptoms of disease in order to find the cause. He also developed many nature-based cures. He was one of the first Western doctors to use tree bark to treat the disease malaria.

Thomas Sydenham

Locke in London

The Earl of Shaftesbury was a wealthy and important man. Through him, Locke made connections. Locke met with political, economic, and scientific groups. In 1668, he became a member of the Royal Society. The Royal Society provided a space for scientists to share their work. They would discuss science and conduct experiments.

Between 1671 and 1675, Locke turned his attention to government and economic systems. During this time, he began work on two drafts. One was his *Two Treatises of Government*. The other was his great work *An Essay Concerning Human Understanding*.

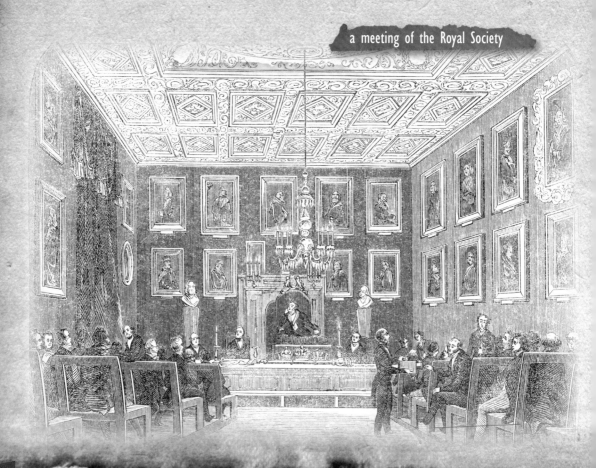

a meeting of the Royal Society

Dissenters of the Church of England

Robert Hooke

Robert Hooke was a member of the Royal Society. He was the first person to suggest that fossils were the imprints of plants and animals from thousands of years ago. This led to the idea of extinction. *Extinction* means that a whole species of plants or animals can die out over time.

John Milton

In 1667, John Milton's *Paradise Lost* retold the biblical story of Adam and Eve. In the story, Milton explores the conflict among free will, intellect, and faith. Like Locke, Milton wondered if people controlled their own lives or if they were driven by forces beyond themselves.

Around this time, Parliament passed a bill. The bill made all English lords pledge an **oath** of loyalty to the Church of England. The earl sympathized with the Dissenters. The Dissenters were those who did not belong to the Church. Because of this, the earl fell from public favor. He could no longer give Locke money.

While at Oxford, Locke had written an essay supporting religious **toleration**. He did not publish the paper. But Locke's views were well known. Locke wanted to avoid conflict with the throne. So, he left for France in 1675.

John Milton

Another Country

Locke had never before traveled abroad. Upon arriving in France, he hired a tutor to help him learn French. He also started a new journal. He was eager to learn more about France and record his impressions.

France was a Roman Catholic country. It was ruled by an all-powerful Catholic, King Louis XIV. Locke's journal reveals his sadness at the way Protestants were treated. Non-Catholics, he noted, could not hold public office. They could not teach at universities or hold public services. However, Locke was inspired by the fact that few of these Protestants abandoned their faith. In the face of so many difficulties, they held strong to their beliefs.

seventeenth-century France

King Louis XIV

Locke found travel enlightening. He liked meeting and speaking with new people. Locke tried to treat everyone he met with the utmost respect. Through his travels, Locke concluded that roadside inns were a better place to learn about life than royal courts.

One of Locke's best friends in France was Nicolas Toinard (toh-NAHR). Toinard was a **devout** Roman Catholic and a scholar of the New Testament. The two men spent hours together. They would debate the nature of man and religion. Despite their differences, they remained friends for the rest of their lives.

René Descartes

The Revolution and the Philosopher

England's Glorious Revolution

In 1679, Locke returned to England. The country was in the middle of a great conflict. King Charles II did not have a son and **heir**. Some feared that the throne would pass to his Catholic nephew, James.

A political group, led by the Earl of Shaftesbury, proposed a bill forbidding Catholics from holding power. To prevent the bill from passing, the king dissolved, or got rid of, Parliament. The earl was accused of treason. He fled to the Netherlands and died a month later. Locke arrived in the Netherlands afterward, in September 1683. He stayed there until 1689.

King James II

The crown is offered to William and Mary.

Charles II died in 1685. James II took the throne and Parliament returned. James was unpopular because of his belief that the king should have absolute power. It was not long before a dispute arose between the king and Parliament over who could make laws.

In 1688, William of Orange, a Dutch Protestant, drove James from the throne. William and his wife Mary were crowned king and queen. One of William's first acts was to sign the Bill of Rights. It was passed by Parliament in 1689. It stated that the king could only rule with the consent of Parliament.

The View from Abroad

Locke had left England just in time to avoid arrest. In 1684, he received a letter. It ordered him to return to London. He was to stand trial for writing treasonous **pamphlets**. He was accused of encouraging others to rebel against the government.

Locke was fearful of being seized. He did not want to be sent back to England. He kept moving from one Dutch city to another. He followed events in England closely through letters from friends. Locke could not join directly in the Glorious Revolution. But, he did give his thoughts on the matter through his letters.

Locke knew that the changes taking place in England were more than political. People were trying to create a new kind of society. Locke began to collect his notes and essays. He wanted to publish them in a book. The subjects he focused on were government, education, and religious toleration.

Most of all, Locke focused on the idea of knowledge itself. How did people know what they did? How did humans understand? These questions became *An Essay Concerning Human Understanding*. This 800-page essay would change western philosophy. It would also change the course of history.

AN

ESSAY

CONCERNING

Human Underſtanding.

BY

JOHN LOCKE, Gent.

The TWELFTH EDITION.

VOLUME II.

LONDON:

Printed for C. HITCH in *Pater-Noster-Row*;
J. PEMBERTON in *Fleet-Street*; J. BEECHCROFT
in *Lombard-Street*; and S. SYMON in *Cornhill*.

MDCCXLI.

Epistemology

Epistemology (ih-pis-tuh-MOL-uh-jee) is the study and theory of knowledge. In particular, it explains how people are able to tell the difference between fact and fiction. Locke's work on human understanding is an example of epistemology.

Queen Mary II

In the years leading up to the Glorious Revolution, many Englishmen fled to the Netherlands. Mary, the queen, was the daughter of King James II. Though her father was Catholic, she was raised Protestant. At 15, she married William of Orange, the Dutch ruler. This created an **alliance** between Dutch and English Protestants. Attractive and outgoing, Mary was popular in both countries.

Queen Mary II

23

Religion and State

When King William and Queen Mary agreed to a **constitutional monarchy**, the Glorious Revolution came to an end. Locke could finally return home to England. In 1689, Locke published two of his major works: *A Letter Concerning Toleration* and *Two Treatises of Government*.

Locke believed that the state should not have a say in religion. Religious beliefs, he said, cannot be forced. The state cannot make people change their innermost beliefs. Locke's views of religious freedom did not include Roman Catholics. Locke feared that Catholics were more loyal to the pope than to England. Still, his ideas were very forward-thinking for his day.

John Locke

Locke scorned the divine right of kings. He liked the idea of the social contract. The government, he said, could only rule with the consent of its citizens. All humans were born free. But they needed some form of authority for society to function. The government's role was to keep the peace. This way society could flourish. Citizens had the right to rebel against a government that broke its own laws.

title page of Locke's *Two Treatises of Government*

TWO TREATISES OF

Government:

In the former,
The *false Principles*, and *Foundation*
OF
Sir ROBERT FILMER,
And his FOLLOWERS,
ARE
Detected and Overthrown.
The latter is an

ESSAY

CONCERNING THE
True Original, Extent, and End
OF
Civil Government.

LONDON,
Printed for *Awnsham Churchill*, at the *Black
Swan* in *Ave-Mary-Lane*, by *Amen-
Corner*, 1690.

Constitutional Monarchy

In a constitutional monarchy, the power of the king and queen is restricted by a constitution. The monarchs shared power with Parliament. After several centuries, the English monarchy's role became largely ceremonial. By the twentieth century, an elected prime minister served as the head of government.

Republic

A republic is a state in which people have the power to elect their own leaders. The name comes from Plato's (PLEY-tohz) *The Republic*. Plato was an Ancient Greek philosopher. Locke did not believe England should be a pure republic, but he did incorporate some of Plato's theories into his work.

Plato

Jean-Jacques Rousseau

One of the philosophers most influenced by Locke was the Frenchman Jean-Jacques Rousseau (zhahn zhahk roo-SOH). Like Locke, Rousseau believed children could be taught through their own experiences. He thought that humans were naturally good. The purpose of education was to develop that goodness.

Gottfried Leibniz

Not all philosophers agreed with Locke. Gottfried Leibniz (GAWT-freet LAHYB-nits), a German philosopher, did not believe the mind was a blank slate, nor did he accept the social contract. He believed that kings needed strong power to repress rebellion.

Unlocking the Mind

Locke's greatest love was education. He said that education was for everyone. Locke believed that children of all social classes were capable of learning. In one of his essays, he describes the mind at birth as a blank slate. Some called this *tabula rasa* (TAB-yuh-luh RAH-suh). He also believed that knowledge comes mainly from direct experience and observation. This theory is known as **empiricism** (em-PIR-uh-siz-uhm).

In 1684, a friend of Locke's had asked how he should educate his son. Locke published his reply to his friend in 1693. Recalling his own school days, Locke wrote that children should not memorize long texts. Rather, they should learn from nature. Science and geography were more relevant than Latin classics. Locke stressed the importance of physical exercise and good nutrition. Children, he claimed, could be taught through discussions. They could learn to reason for themselves. They did not need to be bribed or punished.

Of course, later scientists discovered that the human brain is far from a blank slate at birth. Learning is a more complex process than Locke thought. Yet Locke's theories of human nature helped promote more opportunities for education. Locke "unlocked" the minds of teachers and students for many future generations.

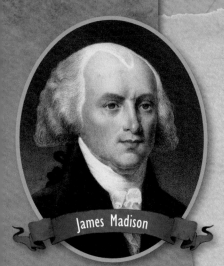

James Madison

James Madison

James Madison, the fourth president of the United States, is also known as the father of the U.S. Constitution. He authored the Bill of Rights, which became the first 10 amendments to the Constitution. The first amendment guarantees freedom of religion, free speech, the right to peaceful assembly, and the right to petition the government—all ideas promoted by John Locke.

The Study of Locke

Locke continues to attract the attention of scholars today. A group of international scholars established the Digital Locke Project in 2003. It made all of Locke's works available on the Internet.

Locke Lives On

By 1695, Locke was one of the most famous men in Europe. He spent the last years of his life reading, writing, and teaching. He did not publish any major works after 1694. But he did keep writing in his journals.

Strangers and friends wrote to him constantly. They wanted his advice. Scientists shared their experiments with him. Sick people asked for medical cures. Parents wanted his help in raising their children. Locke remained alert and active until his death in 1704. He was 72 years old.

a letter from John Locke to a friend, John Sloane

Benjamin Franklin, John Adams, and Thomas Jefferson write the Declaration of Independence.

Nowhere was Locke's influence felt more than in America. Thomas Jefferson called Locke one of the three greatest men who had ever lived. Jefferson wrote in the Declaration of Independence that all men are entitled to "life, liberty, and the pursuit of happiness." His words echoed those of Locke. James Madison made freedom of religion part of the first amendment to the United States Constitution. He was honoring Locke's ideas, as well. Locke was a voice for liberty, freedom, and education for all.

Glossary

alliance—a union between people, families, or groups

barometer—an instrument that measures the pressure of the atmosphere

Cavaliers—a group in England that believed in the absolute power of the king

ceremonial—performing customs and behaviors at an appropriate time

charter—an official document that shows the rights and laws for a group

clerk—a person who keeps records

commonwealth—a group of independent states united by choice for a common objective

constitutional monarchy—a society where the power of the monarchy is limited by a parliament

controversial—something that is heavily debated within society

devout—dedicated to a cause

empiricism—the theory that all knowledge comes from observation and experimentation

Enlightenment—the period of European and American history from roughly 1630 to 1800, which witnessed the development of the scientific revolutions and the growth of democratic ideals

free will—one's own choice or decision

heir—a person who inherits property or a title when someone dies

Latin—a language that was used by the Roman Catholic Church

oath—a sincere promise to a respected person, often promising unity

pacifism—against war or violence

pamphlets—short, printed, and unbound publications with no covers or with paper covers

Parliament—a governing body in the United Kingdom

patron—a person who supports someone with money

philosopher—someone who studies human thought

philosophy—the study of human thought

physicist—a scientist who studies matter and energy

prestigious—important, held in high regard

respiration—the act of breathing

revolution—a dramatic change in society

rural—in the country, far from a large city

scholarship—money given to a student to pay for further education

sermons—religious speeches, usually by a priest, a minister, or a rabbi

toleration—acceptance

treason—the crime of attempting to overthrow the government

Index

Your Turn!

John Locke was an English scholar and philosopher. He dedicated his life to studying many different subjects. During his life, he came up with new ideas about law, medicine, government, education, and the human mind. His ideas about government became the basis for the U.S. Constitution and the Bill of Rights.

Here's My Business Card

Look at the image of John Locke. Beneath his name are the words *Célèbre Philosophe*, which means "celebrated philosopher." Redesign this artwork as a modern-day business card. Create a new job title for Locke. Include a list of Locke's skills, his contact information, and a catchy slogan to promote his services. You could even design a logo for him!

JEAN LOCKE
Célèbre Philosophe.